For Humanity ...
For You

Different Windows to the World

Written by someone with MS

Robert Brett

FOR HUMANITY ... FOR YOU
DIFFERENT WINDOWS TO THE WORLD

iUniverse books may be ordered through booksellers or by contacting:

iUniverse
1663 Liberty Drive
Bloomington, IN 47403
www.iuniverse.com
1-800-Authors (1-800-288-4677)

ISBN: 978-1-5320-3081-9 (sc)
ISBN: 978-1-5320-3082-6 (e)

Library of Congress Control Number: 2017915606

Print information available on the last page.

iUniverse rev. date: 11/10/2017

Dedicated to my family and all those
who need some inspiration.

With thanks to The Bellwoods' Team, Denise,
Vicky, Erez and Corporate Girl for their
support and encouragement

Contents

Contents

About the Book and Author

Life is a funny thing in that it does what it wants, when it wants. It has no limits and doesn't discriminate. It's completely unpredictable. I've had many significant life-altering battles with MS and in the course of coping with its effects, have learned to look at life in different ways. "Different Windows to the World" is about offering fresh perspectives. By opening our mind, it allows us to see what others cannot. It's like viewing the same thing through different windows and seeing it from different angles.

This book evolved through an accumulation of thoughts and insights gained over time through my own personal struggles. With it, I hope to help those feeling down about life, people who cope with major challenges and I wish to offer unique viewpoints. Major challenges could be anything from various life situations to addiction or depression. If anyone is going through difficult times, I want to share some thoughts and tips that I found useful. If I can help one person, that will be the reward.

Prologue

I discussed some of the book's content with a friend and was surprised to hear that she felt the same way about things. She went through very difficult times coping with various pressures and strains, so it confirmed for me that others had similar thoughts. It seems that people facing significant challenges in their lives seem to discover comparable thoughts about life. I want to offer my thoughts and philosophies to everyone, including people who haven't had to travel similar routes, so they can avoid having to go through very difficult times. This book is for everyone. While some of my experiences involve disability, the underlying message is universal. It's not the problems that define us, it's how we choose to handle them. It seems that it takes getting very low to experience a clarity of life. For me, it stripped everything down to the basics and all I saw was what's really important. The one thing I wanted to do is help people avoid having to get so low that they experience similar feelings or to boost the spirits of those already in a dark place.

- *Chapter 1* -

<u>Thoughts</u>

"A man is but the product of his thoughts. What he
thinks, he becomes."
- Gandhi

I strongly believed in myself and had the confidence to deal
with anything. I found that there are three keys to happiness:
acceptance, flexibility and an open mind.

Acceptance:
- I had to work at finding ways to accept various situations
  and it really tested my inner strength. This involved
  adapting to my new environments, exploring possible
  options and being creative in balancing needs with
  what's available.
- When life changes are permanent, staying upset won't
  change anything. It's natural to mourn, but be aware
  that time and life are still moving forward. A lot of people
  wish they could extend the time they have in this world,
  so embrace the time you still have. I saw people waste
  years feeling sad about their circumstances, only to
  emerge feeling better after accepting things.
- Like with my new circumstances, I treated my changed
  life as a project and worked with various organizations
  to find out about what's available. You may find that in
  some situations, a simple change is all that's needed.
  While in others, a more drastic approach is necessary.
  I've also found that sometimes a drastic change helps
  by shaking things up. I would always begin by thinking

of one thing to do differently. "A journey of a thousand miles begins with a single step."

- I realized that the more I accepted things, the easier life became. It wasn't a question of whether I liked the changes or not, I had to learn to live within changing boundaries. Although disability was the reason that things were changing, I spent years trying to keep life moving in the same exact direction and wasted a lot of time and effort struggling.

Flexibility:

- Life is full of choices and when faced with something, sometimes the hard road is the best road. This may not be the popular option because of the difficulty it presents, but the end result may be better. Like they say, "the end may justify the means."
- In life, things happen ... Any disability is challenging, whether sudden or progressive, and it requires that you adapt to your situation. You may have been able to do things one way in the past, but you may find that you can no longer do things that way anymore. You can forever grieve the loss of what you used to be able to do or you can learn about the ways in which you can do things now. There is a lot to learn about your new situation and you'll develop little strategies as you go.

"We cannot change the cards we are dealt, just how we play the hand."
- Randy Pausch

- It's true what is said about life, "you never stop learning." It takes courage to accept your new situation and its limitations, but the important thing is to keep moving forward. It's hard, but be defiant and show life that you can't be beaten. They say that, "true strength comes from within."

- There comes a point in our lives when we have to stop thinking that life's going to be the way we want it to be and start seeing things for how they really are

Personal story:

My ex-wife was amazing and did a lot for me, even at her own health expense. That included doing the cooking, cleaning, laundry, grocery shopping and being a handyman extraordinaire. All this while working full-time and completing a PhD.

She seemed superhuman, pushing her body to the limit and doing the work of multiple people. These numerous responsibilities began to affect her both physically and emotionally. She was normally a very healthy person who was always full of energy, but she began to battle fatigue, became anemic and developed infections more frequently. Coping with all of this also meant a high level of stress and watching her slowly fall apart was unbearable. While it's incredibly difficult to have a disease like this, it's just as hard on the caregiver.

My thinking was this, "MS has destroyed one life, but it stops there!" We discussed things and I told her that I saw what MS was doing to her and that I wanted to take it out of her life. That meant going our separate ways. She understood my position and was thankful. It was the hardest thing I've ever done, but it was the right thing to do in our situation. Like the saying goes, "If you love something, set it free."

It was the beginning of a new life in the unknown world of disability and I had to discover all the resources that were available to me. I also felt better seeing her move onto a new and healthier chapter of her life. Moving into this new world was like running into a thick fog where I couldn't see anything and many things were unfamiliar. I was uncertain of what lay ahead, but would deal with things as they came. I explored my new surroundings and found things that were helpful to me. Eventually, I emerged on the other side of this fog only to see that life for both of us was better. The unforeseen outcome of an incredibly difficult decision turned out to be better in the end.

Randy Pausch, who wrote "The Last Lecture" for his family before his passing. I highly recommend this book. I first learned about him from Oprah and again on youtube.com ... fascinating guy!

As people, we're all the same, but we're all different. We're all the same in that everyone is dealing with his or her own challenges. We're all different because we face diverse personal issues. As Plato once said, "be kind, for everyone you meet is fighting a hard battle." We're as individual as our fingerprints, but as different as our personalities and that's what makes everyone special and unique.

Our lives are a combination of personal experiences and inherent characteristics. How you handle things is what matters and that says a lot about you.

It's important to acknowledge and celebrate your achievements. It's common to solve one problem and focus on the next, without taking a breath in between. In doing so, it becomes easy to forget about your accomplishments. After each, reward yourself by taking some time, even if it's only an hour or two.

For example, a friend's lease was ending and she didn't want to renew. She was desperately searching for another apartment to rent, as she had no other options. After spending a lot of time looking, she found the perfect place.

She then worked hard to leave nothing but positive impressions with the landlord, without seeming like she desperately wanted it. Knowing that there were other interested parties, the waiting period for a decision caused her immense stress. Luckily, she was offered the place.

Typically, her mind quickly moved onto the next task of painting rooms. Reflecting on her desperate situation, being offered the apartment meant that she had avoided having to deal with some difficult problems. Considering the amount of effort she put into this and the stress it caused, getting the apartment was a major achievement and that success should be celebrated.

Think about these thoughts on money ...

- Some people too often put money first, where it's always about the most bang for the buck. I agree that money is important, but there are times when foregoing a sale and paying regular price may make life easier than what the deal is worth. I'm considering the effect it has on all aspects of a person's life, like stress, inconvenience, time, etc.

- Sometimes it seems as though people put money ahead of common sense.

Who knows how limited our time is, so do your best to make your life a good one! That includes your influence on others and the lives you affect. Thinking about this helped me through things. I wanted to be an inspiration for those around me during difficult times of their own. By dealing with my major challenges with disability, people will remember my efforts.

In keeping with the thought of time, our lives may be as short as twenty years or as long as ninety. It's up to each of us as to how we spend them.

I don't believe in forcing things. Often, it doesn't lead to anything good and you may not get the expected results. Whether you're dealing with something tangible or not, forcing something may do more harm than good and may cause more problems.

I find life to be easiest when letting things happen naturally, instead of forcing things. More often than not, it leads to something better. Doing things this way allows for new options and opportunities to present themselves.

Each person has their own definition of the awe-inspiring human spirit, but they all share some common thoughts and qualities. Its unstoppable drive pushes us to overcome great obstacles and accomplish what seems impossible. It possesses a desire to keep moving forward and to excel. Just some of the human qualities it controls are personality, passion, emotion, motivation, will and willpower.

The Human Spirit is also responsible for our selfless actions and makes us want to help others. It gives people the ability to fight oppression, adversity and fight for what's right. Like when an army fights for others against an enemy. An example of this can be seen when looking at the United Nations and Human Rights.

Life is all about perspective and not comparison, but it's human nature to weigh ourselves against others. It can be either of the healthy kind or the harmful type. Good comparison keeps us motivated, makes us strive for things and encourages you to better yourself. It feeds your ambition and pushes you to achieve.

Comparing yourself to others can also have negative effects. It may lower your self-esteem and self-confidence with feelings of inferiority. It can erode the desire to achieve and possibly lead to depression. Comparison is like having an angel on one shoulder and the devil on the other.

Some have a good understanding of life and what's important. It's the people in our lives, playing key roles and helping us along our journey through life. When a few authors, myself included, have reflected on life, the main message is consistently that things don't matter, people do. I wanted to compare life to something simple and nothing illustrates it better than an onion. For obvious reasons, I had reservations in doing so. If you keep peeling away the layers, eventually you'll reach the core. Think of the layers as being material things like houses, cars and boats and the core being central things like family and friends. By looking at life this way, you see what's really important. You focus less on monetary things and see disagreements as trivial. With this new view of life, the answers to some problems may be easier to see. Some describe it as a moment of clarity and it can lead to a feeling of euphoria. In speaking to others, this seems to be discovered at a very low point in one's life.

Recap

In this chapter, we looked at the three keys to happiness being acceptance, flexibility and an open mind.

- sometimes the hard road is the best road
- be defiant and show life that you can't be beaten
- celebrate your achievements and reward yourself by taking some time, even if it's only an hour or two
- I find life to be easiest when letting things happen naturally
- things don't matter, people do
- life is like an onion, where the layers represent material things and the core represents personal things

Looking Ahead

In the next chapter, I'll discuss Positive Thinking.

- Chapter 2 -

Positive Thinking

Question: Where can you find inspiration?
Like anything, it takes a conscious effort to be aware of inspiration. By that, I mean you have to internalize it and make a mental note so as not to forget it. It's not enough to just look at something inspiring, really see it. Inspiration is easy to find because it's around us all the time. It's in the news, our lives, peoples' stories, the arts, sports.

When dealing with people, I'm conscious of how I come across. I put myself in their shoes. Empathize and be aware of your attitude and behaviour. Treat others how you would want to be treated. Goodness will be rewarded and smiles will pay you back.

"Good actions give strength to ourselves and inspire good actions in others."
- Plato

Focusing on negatives is too easy and is an easy trap to fall into, which only re-enforces why you hate your situation. Soon, all you see are negatives. In this way, only you create barriers for yourself. It may be difficult to see, but if you look hard enough there is always something positive that can be found. Challenge yourself to think of a positive by looking at things differently. Thinking of only negative things has the same effect as trying to walk through sludge

"An optimist sees an opportunity in every calamity; a pessimist sees a calamity in every opportunity."
- Winston Churchill

Having a positive State of Mind will help you to meet challenges, convey self-confidence and others will see you in a positive light. It can only help when you have a positive "can do" attitude and when you remain upbeat. Having a negative one will see you struggling and battling against things more often.

Several studies have found that optimism does lead to greater happiness and longevity. If you have an optimistic state of mind, you're better able to cope with stresses and can take on life challenges more resiliently.

A 20-year study of over 1,700 older men conducted by the Harvard School of Public Health found that worry about social conditions, health and personal finances all significantly increased the risk of coronary heart disease.

Be a good person ... your life may be hard, but that doesn't mean you have to treat everybody else that way. I firmly believe that if you're nice to people, they will respond to others in the same way. Maybe not today, but over time. By doing this, you build a positive impression of you in peoples' minds and you'll find that others will want to help you in the same way that you help others. "Actions speak louder than words."

Dream big, but stay grounded and be realistic. Follow your dreams. I love this quote by Les Brown

"Shoot for the moon. Even if you miss, you'll land amongst the stars."
- Les Brown

As much as possible, don't let life revolve around your struggles. As difficult as things may be, force yourself to think of a way to adapt. Don't worry about social norms ... just do what you can. I have Progressive MS, which has made life a constant battle. I could look at it negatively and think of all the things it has taken away and yet will. This would only result in feelings of anger towards the past and fear for the future. Or, I could look at it positively by thinking, "okay, I still have the use of my hands, so I should enjoy that ability while it lasts and go out to a restaurant." This is one thing that MS has taught me.

You never know if and when an illness or accident may occur. It's important to enjoy those around you and life in general. Don't wait too long to do things, as you risk having them overshadowed by other things and it's not long until they fade into the background, perhaps forgotten altogether

"Never leave that 'til tomorrow which you can do today."
- Benjamin Franklin

Life Tip:
Learn to live before it's too late. Enjoy the present, not the past. Just don't procrastinate too much.

I wish to highlight the importance of a positive attitude. In life, attitude is everything, so don't dwell on things. You'll only bring yourself and those around you down with feelings of sadness.

Life is already difficult and you owe it to yourself to not make things harder.

"Attitude is a little thing that makes a big difference."
- Winston Churchill

The glass half full/empty analogy: When a person sees that the glass is half full, they are appreciating what's there. When a person sees it as half empty, they are comparing it to a full glass and see only what's missing.
Along with the previous point about not making things harder for yourself, appreciate what's already there. Positive thinking is not only about the things you do, but also how you see things.

It's fine to be idealistic, but you also need to be realistic. If you aren't, always being too positive means you have further to fall back to reality and it may be tough on yourself

Train your mind by making a conscious effort to see things positively. Challenge yourself by asking how you can look at a situation in a different way? For example, when something triggers an angry emotion in you. Stop ... over time, this will become an unconscious habit

Moving uproots you with packing and unpacking, finances and much more. It's hard for these reasons. You can look at things positively or negatively. Think of it like an adventure, somewhere new to explore. Bringing with it new experiences and learning. Do this whether it's new or even though you may have dealt with it in the past, look at things from a different angle.

When it comes to anger, don't take the bait! As soon as you or someone else gets angry during a disagreement, that person will have failed to make their point heard. Sometimes, it's hard to avoid being provoked and irritated, but the winner of an argument will be the person who can remain calm and unruffled. Step back from things to gain some perspective on the real size and importance of the issue. In the grand scheme of things, it may not be worth putting yourself through the anger, agitation and other emotions. Cooler heads will prevail!

Don't complain too often and become known as a complainer or grumbler.
Dictionary.com describes Grumbling as an expression of discontent; complaint; unhappy murmur; growl.
Synonyms: irritable, grouchy

Some absolute barriers exist in your environment, both physical and those created by others, which may be out of your control. Others are self-imposed and exist due to a resiliency to change. Change can be difficult, but challenge yourself to look for a positive side. Because I don't like seeing myself fail, I strive to achieve a goal. If looking at something negatively only leads to anger or frustration, that is doing nothing good for me. I'm driven to avoid making my life hard, so I try to find a positive way of looking at something.

I don't fear change, in fact, I embrace it. I always look at it as a challenge that is full of opportunity. It consists of investigation, thinking and discovery, kind of like solving a puzzle.

I've always thought this way and my mindset has been the same in all aspects of life, be it personal or professional. I treat things like projects, where I'm given a situation, the confines and the objective, I must find the tools needed and search for what is available that can help me

"In the middle of difficulty lies opportunity."
- Albert Einstein

Recap

- Inspiration is around us all the time
- Treat others how you want others to treat you
- Think of a positive by looking at things differently.
- An optimistic mind will help you with stress and challenges
- Be a good person and others will want to help you
- Don't worry about social norms … just do what you can
- Enjoy those around you
- Enjoy the present, not the past
- Attitude is everything
- Don't let life revolve around your struggles
- Glass is half full: appreciating what's there

- Step back and gain some perspective on the real size and importance of the issue
- Don't become known as a complainer or a grumbler

Looking Ahead

In the next chapter, I'll go into some Philosophies.

- *Chapter 3* -

<u>Philosophies</u>

Life can be compared to many things, but to me, it resembles being in a rowboat floating on the ocean. Like the waves, it's filled with ups and downs, sometimes calm and sometimes turbulent. The current can be strong and pull you off course from where you wanted to go. It's natural to keep paddling towards a specific destination, but the current may be overwhelming and you soon realize that maintaining that course is futile. Look up, scan the horizon and select a new destination in line with where you're being pulled. Unexpected things may happen that force you to change direction from where you were going with your life.

In the same way that you would ride the waves and guide the boat ashore, try acting similarly with life. Instead of struggling against something, just go with it and let life lead. You may be surprised at where it takes you, but by being flexible and keeping an open mind, you may also find yourself in a place where opportunities abound.

For the most part, take control of your life and guide it where you want it to go, but don't force life to go a certain way. There may be some instances where you should relinquish control and let life lead and others where you have to drastically change where it's headed.

As mentioned by others, visualize where you are and where you want to go. I have found this to be an important way to achieve desired results.

LifeTips7_Envision:
Throughout life, we find ourselves confronted with very difficult choices and situations. I found that by envisioning where I wanted to be helped to make any upcoming hurdles easier and less daunting. I wasn't concerned about each of the many challenges that lay ahead because I knew that I was moving in the right direction.

Although it's good to know about things in advance so you can think about the best way forward, life doesn't always work that way. Because you can't always predict things, I've found the best way to learn about a situation is by just going through it.

Look at where you are and where you want to be. Don't overwhelm yourself by trying to figure out the "how to's" in between these two points, as there will be many unpredictable situations in front of you. Just go through things taking baby steps, dealing with one thing at a time. Let the idea of where you want to be guide your actions. Breaking a big task like this into smaller more manageable pieces will make things less overwhelming. At least, you can be assured that you are moving in the right direction.

There are many times that envisioning something has been a very helpful tool to determine how to proceed with a situation.

Recap

In this chapter, we considered visualization, something I consider to be extremely valuable. We also looked at different ways of looking at life.

- visualize where you are and where you want to go. I have found this to be an important way to achieve desired results

- Life resembles being in a rowboat floating on the ocean.
- Select a new destination in line with where you're being pulled.
- Things may happen that force you to change direction from where you were going with your life.
- With life, instead of always struggling against things, once-in-a-while just go with it and let life lead.
- Don't force life to go a certain way
  To do this, guide life in the right direction
- I've found the best way to learn about a situation is by just going through it.
- Don't overwhelm yourself by trying to figure out the "how to's
- Just go through things taking baby steps, dealing with one thing at a time
- Breaking a big task like this into smaller more manageable pieces will make things less daunting.

Looking Ahead

In the next chapter, I'll examine Life's Path.

- *Chapter 4* -

Life's Path

I believe that life is unexpected and unpredictable. The unknown is what makes it an emotional, challenging and interesting journey. When I reflect on certain aspects of my life, I wouldn't have foreseen the many twists and turns it has taken. Life is always changing and brings with it unexpected situations, so it's easiest and quickest just to go with it and adapt on-the-fly

- We stand on the shoulders of giants and see further, building on previous discoveries

"If I have seen further it is by standing on the shoulders of Giants."
- Isaac Newton

Direct and steer your own life, no-one else but you is responsible for its path and direction. You don't have to know exactly where you're going, just as long as you keep moving forward in the right direction. Life is not about the destination, but the journey along the way. Like they say, "stop and smell the roses."

The road you travel is built by you and you choose the destination where it leads. Everyone's on their own path and the choices you make define who you are. Life is your own story that is constantly being written.

Recap

In this chapter, we talked about life being nonlinear and a good way to handle things.

- Direct your life where you want it to go
- Everyone chooses where their life goes

Looking Ahead

In the next chapter, I'll explore different Obstacles and Barriers.

- Chapter 5 -

Obstacles and Barriers

- Barriers can be overcome by making hard decisions
- They can be caused by ourselves. Your mind creates barriers.
- Life is only as difficult and complex as you make it.
- Often, it's people themselves who make their lives difficult with their own actions.

The dictionary defines fear as a distressing emotion aroused by impending danger, whether the threat is real or imagined. When you work at facing your fears, you'll notice the fading of barriers in your path towards achievement.

Recap

In this chapter, we looked at barriers.

- Your mind creates barriers.
- Life is only as difficult and complex as you make it.
- Often, it's people themselves who make their lives difficult with their own actions.
- When you work at facing your fears, you'll notice the fading of barriers in your way

Looking Ahead

In the next chapter, I'll talk about characteristics that I've found helpful.

- *Chapter 6* -

<u>Helpful Personal Characteristics</u>

Throughout my life, a few personal characteristics have been very helpful to me. Determination and persistence are significant attributes that have allowed me to open many doors and venture down many paths. They have helped to greatly expand my horizons.

When I see something that is important to me, I gather all my resources and try hard to achieve it. During this time, my determination is like an unending well. Together with persistence, nothing is unattainable. I take the attitude of "I can achieve ...", it's just a matter of figuring out how best to go about it. In many situations, the only thing that can stop a person is themselves. Determination and persistence fuel a fire inside me to not give-up. It's that unstoppable drive of the human spirit.

Life constantly challenges a person to re-evaluate situations. I was interviewing for a particular job and it came down to two of us. In the end, I wasn't offered the position. The natural reaction would have been to feel unhappy or disappointed, but I looked at it another way. Sure, I could have done the job and would have liked it, but in addition to coping with a disability, it would have significantly added to my stress level and my overall health would have suffered. Instead, I had an opportunity to work on this book at home. I discovered many benefits that I wouldn't have otherwise thought about and it revealed certain things that would have been difficult. I find that the more flexible you can be with life, the easier it is.

I also rely on creative thinking a lot. When looking at a problem, I see it from various angles and think of different ways to approach it. With disability, if I can't do something the same way as others, I make it a challenge instead of a barrier. I challenge myself to think of other ways to achieve the same result. It's not what you can't do, it's HOW you can do it another way?

Having an open mind gives you many more possibilities to consider when thinking of things in new ways. Be aware that the mind can create its own barriers. You may not want to do something for a certain reason, so it's automatically rejected. Examine that reason and ask yourself if the end justifies the means? You may be surprised to find that it wasn't as bad as you thought it would be. Without an open mind, you will miss some opportunities

Flexibility is to be adaptable to changing situations, creative thinking is to generate new possibilities and open mindedness is to be receptive to new ideas. These three things work together to make you as agile as possible and help when tackling anything that life throws your way.

Self-confidence is a very important quality to have in life. Confidence breeds trust and people want to be around those who are confident in themselves, but not in a conceited way. They'll want to involve you in more and your network of people will expand, bringing with it new opportunities. Things will seem to be gravitating towards you.

"The history of the world is full of men who rose to leadership, by sheer force of self-confidence, bravery and tenacity."
- Mahatma Gandhi

It incites a belief in yourself, which is a strong quality that radiates from a person. To others, it conveys a sense of trust.

It's something that can't be taught, only gained through your experiences. Self-confidence helps you to speak-up in a crowd when you have important things to say. Everyone has their insecurities, but they fade into the background as you become increasingly confident. With it, you'll feel more comfortable with yourself. Part of building confidence is that you have to try things without fearing failure. Sometimes things work and sometimes they don't, but you won't know until you try. If something doesn't work, at least you've tried and you'll know for next time. Don't fear failure, learn from it instead. Just as important is to not dwell on things. Your self-esteem will take a beating and you run the risk of not wanting to try again. Remember that people make mistakes, that is how we learn and each person is different. Being successful at something may mean attempting it several times until you get it right. Learn not to care what others think of you.

"Success consists of going from failure to failure without loss of enthusiasm."
- Winston Churchill

Being laid-back really helps to accommodate others and give them more time to do things for you. Relax your expectations and realize that certain time constraints may be self-imposed and adjustable, unless it's life or death. In relation to that, it may not be as extreme as you think. That's not to say it's not urgent, but it might help you to see it differently and allow for some flexibility. That will reduce your stress level. Try practicing this in other situations. Life should be easy, not hard.

By combining these qualities, I'm armed with some highly effective tools to help successfully navigate situations.

Recap

In this chapter, we discussed characteristics that I've found helpful.

- Determination and persistence are significant attributes that have helped to greatly expand my possibilities
- In many situations, the only thing that can stop a person is themselves
- The more flexible you can be with life, the easier it is.
- See a problem from various angles and think of different ways to approach it
- Flexibility is to be adaptable to changing situations, creative thinking is to generate new possibilities and open mindedness is to be receptive to new ideas.
- Without an open mind, you will miss some opportunities
- Self-confidence is a very important quality to have in life
- You have to try things without fearing failure, you won't know until you try
- People make mistakes, that is how we learn and each person is different
- Don't dwell on things
- Learn not to care what others think of you.
- Life should be easy, not hard
- Relax your expectations

Looking Ahead

In the next chapter, I'll look at Society and its effects.

- *Chapter 7* -

Society and Expectations

Society has framed life with certain expectations for a "perfect life". Because of this, people set the bar extremely high for themselves. Things become difficult when trying to manage these expectations and other social pressures. One of the main stresses in life is that people feel they have to meet these numerous demands. When comparing their lives to this, if they don't reach a certain target, it could lead to much unhappiness and depression. Don't live your life according to Society, it's expectations must be tailored to you.

We are extremely hard on ourselves and judge our lives against these difficult standards. If we don't achieve them, we feel like failures. This is a good example of how we are our own worst enemy. We make life hard by trying to live up to these ideals. We try to do everything, but are often too busy to notice life going by.

Regarding making life unnecessarily difficult, it's easy to suffer from the "Keeping up with the Joneses" syndrome. It's a nasty bug that affects millions. People care about their standard of living relative to others in society. It creates an insatiable appetite for material goods in order to express their socioeconomic status. We're so focused on our own lives and what we want next. Consumerism has fueled the need for more money and the next thing. We need to place more importance on our connections with family and friends.

Blessed is he who expects nothing, for he shall never be disappointed.
- Attributed to both Jonathan Swift and Benjamin Franklin

Lower your expectations, but strive for excellence. By constantly giving things your best effort, you can always be confident in what you've done to achieve things.

For some, life is challenging (ex. illness), but for others, they make their lives unnecessarily difficult. To those with a disability, realize and try to accept that your life is very different from others. By not accepting things, life will be full of disappointment. Also, you can't use the same measuring stick as everyone else to judge your performance. That's not right and only you can avoid this.

In my life, I wanted to be completely independent and avoided asking for help, even though I knew that people were more than happy to give any assistance. Disability freed me from this stubborn thinking and now I find it easy to ask, "excuse me, can you ... for me?" Look at it this way, your situation is a free pass to ask for help.

One definition of optimism is to anticipate the best possible outcome. This is good as long as "anticipate" does not become "expect".

Unconsciously, sometimes I focused on the negative outcomes of small and insignificant situations. I would shake my head, laugh and attribute it to Murphy's Law, where if anything can go wrong, it will. It's important to balance life by remembering the positives of similar small situations. When researching things, I had to laugh at this one, "Smile ... tomorrow will be worse."

When looking at Society, it has both good and bad qualities. On the good side, Society gives structure and order to our lives. It does so through laws, the justice system, human rights, equality and it guides people's behaviour regarding what is and isn't acceptable.

People are motivated by improving themselves and through healthy competition with one another, which drives ambition. It is through Society that we develop our mannerisms, it teaches us courtesy and compassion, we learn responsibility, it shows us how to interact with others and it shows us inclusiveness and acceptance.

Also, I've found that there is so much available to people from all levels of government in the Society where I live. You just have to research what exists.

In a perfect world these things would be enough, but there are many exceptions. Some examples are greed, fear, violence, drugs and selfishness

Recap

In this chapter, we talked about Society.

- Don't live your life according to Society, it's expectations must be tailored to you
- We try to do everything, but are often too busy to notice life going by
- Consumerism vs family & friends
- Lower your expectations, but strive for excellence
- People make their lives unnecessarily difficult
- Don't avoid asking for help
- For best outcomes, don't let anticipate become expect
- Remember the positives of situations
- Society gives structure and order to our lives
- There are also some negatives like greed, fear, violence, drugs and selfishness

In the next chapter, I'll offer some life tips.

- *Chapter 8* -

Life Tips

LifeTips1_Live
- Have fun in life and learn to live before your circumstances change.

LifeTips2_Busy
- Don't let your life become constantly busy. In life, be sure to stop and smell the roses. Our lives are very busy and full of daily stresses where it's "necessary" to do everything in as little time as possible, because there's more to do … It's hard to gain an understanding of life amidst all this chaos. Be good to yourself and make a point of taking constant breaks.

LifeTips3_Perspective
- Take a step back and you may find that what you think are big things are really not as big as you thought.

LifeTips4_Moments
- In life, don't miss a moment. Life is a collection of moments.

LifeTips5_Unpredictable
- Remember that in life, anything can happen at any time.

LifeTips6_Key Memory
- It is very important to keep at least one strong thought or memory top-of-mind. Take some time to really think about one and then write it down. Whenever you need some inspiration and perspective, it will be readily available.

LifeTips7_Envision

- Personally, I've found this to be an extremely important and helpful way of looking at life when confronted with difficult situations.

LifeTips8_Consequences

- Always think about possible/worst-case-scenario consequences of your actions

LifeTips9_Important1

- Never forget how you saw things when you were young, your dreams/imagination/passion.
- It's important to laugh.
- Sometimes it's good to let your creativity run free in your mind.
- Sometimes it's good to just forget the world.

LifeTips11_Comparing

- People often compare themselves to others. This should never be done because everyone's different and have different issues affecting their lives. Trying to compare people is like trying to compare apples and oranges.

LifeTips12_Flexibility

- Be flexible with your long-term planning. Set goals and work towards them, but if something gets in the way, adjust your plans to fit your situation.
- Teach yourself to be flexible with goals and timing.
- If you are not flexible and something prevents or prolongs their achievement, it could lead to disappointment and/ or depression.
- Along with acceptance, flexibility is another key to making life easier.

LifeTips13_Career
- In your career, do what you love and the money will follow.
- Be aware of the future, but just concentrate on the present.
- In your life, the most important thing you can do is to take care of you, otherwise your future can be at risk.

LifeTips14_Failure
- It's important to not fear failure, learn from it instead.

LifeTips15_Sights

- Don't set your sights too high.
- If your expectations don't happen, you'll limit your fall to the ground.

LifeTips16_Important2
- In life, have certain aspirations, ambitions and things you want to do.
- Don't pin these down with a date, let them float around in your mind until the opportunity presents itself.

LifeTips17_Best/Worst
- Hope for the best, but plan for the worst
- By that I mean be wise and hope for a positive outcome, but prepare for things if they don't go as planned.

- *Chapter 9* -

Quotes

a. Famous Quote1:

    Never leave that 'til tomorrow which you can do today.

- Benjamin Franklin

b. Favourite Quote1:

    An optimist sees an opportunity in every calamity; a pessimist sees a calamity in every opportunity.

- Winston Churchill

c. Favourite Quote2:

    Shoot for the moon. Even if you miss, you'll land amongst the stars.

- Les Brown

d. Favourite Quote3

    When one door closes, another door opens, but we so often look so long and so regretfully upon the closed door, that we do not see the ones which open for us.

- Alexander Graham Bell

e. Famous Quote2

    Attitude is a little thing that makes a big difference.

- Winston Churchill

f. Famous Quote3

> Blessed is he who expects nothing, for he shall never be disappointed.
>
> > \- Attributed to both Jonathan Swift and Benjamin Franklin

g. Famous Quote4

> A man is but the product of his thoughts. What he thinks, he becomes.
>
> > \- Mahatma Gandhi

h. Famous Quote5

> Any man may easily do harm, but not every man can do good to another.
> Be kind, for everyone you meet is fighting a hard battle.
> Good actions give strength to ourselves and inspire good actions in others.
>
> > \- Plato

i. Famous Quote6

> The only disability in life is a bad attitude.
>
> > \- Scott Hamilton

j. Famous Quote7

> In the middle of difficulty lies opportunity.
>
> > \- Albert Einstein

k. Famous Quote8

> A journey of a thousand miles begins with a single step.
>
> > \- Lao Tzu

l. Famous Quote9

> The history of the world is full of men who rose
> to leadership, by sheer force of self-confidence,
> bravery and tenacity.
>
> > - Mahatma Gandhi

m. Famous Quote10

> Strength does not come from physical capacity,
> it comes from an indomitable will.
>
> > - Mahatma Gandhi

n. Famous Quote11

> We make a living by what we get. We make a
> life by what we give.
>
> > - Winston Churchill

o. Famous Quote12

> Believe you can and you're halfway there.
>
> > - Theodore Roosevelt

p. Famous Quote13

> Life is really simple, but we insist on making it
> complicated.
>
> > - Confucius

q. Famous Quote14

> Anything's possible if you try; dreams are made
> possible if you try.
>
> > - Terry Fox

r. Famous Quote15

> You should never let your fears prevent you
> from doing what you know is 90right.
>
> > - Aung San Suu Kyi

s. Famous Quote16

> We cannot change the cards we are dealt, just how we play the hand.
>
> - Randy Pausch

s. Famous Quote17

> Success consists of going from failure to failure without loss of enthusiasm.
>
> - Winston Churchill

- End -

- When looking at life, it's important to balance seriousness with light heartedness. Personally, in addition to taking some things seriously, I look at life with a cheeky grin.
- If things are frustrating and you think "are you kidding me?", that's a perfect time to stop, step back and look at how someone else might see the situation as humorous.
- Put your emotions into perspective. You may realize that the thing causing your emotions to flare is so small and insignificant in the grand scheme of things.
- I hope this book has provided you with some useful insights.
- Life is constant in that it presents everyone with challenges. If you look at it on a basic level, life is easy. Just treat others the same way that you would want to be treated and remember the onion comparison.

About the Author

Robert Brett has had numerous life-altering battles with Multiple Sclerosis. As a result, he has learned to look at and approach life differently. He wrote this book to help others coping with major life challenges. Robert currently lives in Toronto, Ontario, Canada.

Have Fun and
Enjoy Life

Printed in the United States
By Bookmasters